DOMUS: A JOURNEY INTO ITALY'S MOST CREATIVE INTERIORS

DOMUS

A JOURNEY INTO ITALY'S MOST CREATIVE INTERIORS

OBERTO GILI

MARELLA CARACCIOLO CHIA

RIZZOLI
NEW YORK

New York · Paris · London · Milan

CONTENTS

FOREWORD

"Nothing can be compared to the new life that the discovery of another country provides for a thoughtful person. Although I am still the same I believe to have changed to the bones." –Johann Wolfgang von Goethe, *Italian Journey*

From 1786 to 1788, Goethe embarked on his grand tour of Italy. It took me much longer to complete my own version, which you will see illustrated in this book. With the help of my dear friend Marellina, I visited extraordinary homes, monuments, and landscapes and met the most interesting people.

Quoting Goethe one more time: "I myself must also say I believe it is true that in the end humanitarianism will triumph; only I fear that at the same time the world will be one big hospital and each person will be the other person's humane keeper." Humanitarianism did triumph in Italy together with vulgarity and banality. Everybody is copying what is trendy, fashionable, and cool—far too often disregarding their roots, culture, and history. Thankfully, there still exists a strong minority who beautifully manage to avoid falling in with the flock. They live with tremendous authenticity and creativity by embracing their history and cultivating their own culture that reflects their personalities. This idea of style and living was once rampant in Italy and you will see that it is still ever present in today's society, but only now it is hidden like a private treasure that has to be discovered in a slow and intentional way—much like the process it took to conceive and create it. Style cannot be bought or mass-produced. Here are our finds from Venice to Sicily. I hope this will inspire you to begin your own grand tour, wherever in the world you find yourself.　　　　　　　　–O. G.

MARELLA CARACCIOLO CHIA
A PRIVATE RENAISSANCE

Some rooms—like the pages of a personal diary or scrapbook, or the stage sets of a play—are spaces in constant flux, permeated by the aspirations, the talents, and sometimes even the failures of the individuals who inhabit them. In the course of nearly thirty years discovering and writing about Italian interiors, a good portion of which were photographed by Oberto Gili, I have seen thousands of rooms all over the country. Many of them were exercises in theatrical opulence, others were oases of comfort and domestic pleasures. Room after room, I kept trying to pin down what it was that made some of these spaces, compared to others, so absolutely and irresistibly alive. Was it the eclectic mix of objects? Eclecticism, of course, implies choice and knowledge, but that alone was not it. Was it the classic harmony one associates with great Italian interiors? Or the ever-present sense of history resonating in every nook and cranny? These are important elements, for sure, but alone they did not explain that mysterious alchemy that made some rooms conquer such a special place in my memories. One fundamental thing these particular rooms had in common, I eventually realized, was that they were all absolutely necessary and vital to the life, talent, and, sometimes, obsessions of those who made them. In other words, these interiors told a story.

The concept of rooms that reveal a good story is what this book is essentially about. Oberto Gili and I started talking about recording our "journey" through these "narrative interiors" ever since we met in 1993 during a shoot in Montalcino, Tuscany. In the course of the following two decades, sometimes working side by side for magazine features or on book projects, we traveled all over the country, visiting gardens, villas, castles, city homes, and rural estates. We discovered many beautiful interiors but what stayed with us were the ones belonging to highly creative individuals. *Domus* pays tribute to Italy's centuries-old tradition of using arts and crafts to create masterful interiors. It is the recording of our excursions into the private worlds of a number of artists, craftspeople, gardeners, and connoisseurs living in Italy today.

Our journey, in the book, begins in the northwest of the country, Turin, and zigzags its way across as we progressed southward. We stopped in most of the large cities along the way: Venice, Milan, Florence, Rome, Naples, and Palermo. We also explored rural areas, such as the hilly regions of the Apennines; the Umbrian hills; Maremma, along the coast of Tuscany; the Tuscia region in Lazio, with its wealth of Renaissance palaces and gardens; then down through the wild, rugged region of Puglia; and all the way to Salento, on the very tip of Italy's heel before heading to Sicily. Along the way we visited many artists. People like Luigi Ontani, who transformed a late nineteenth-century cottage into a shrine devoted to his unique take on applied arts, or Maro Gorky and Matthew Spender, who have turned their eighteenth-century farmhouse in Chianti into an Italianate version of the Bloomsbury group's Charleston—filled with frescoed walls, painted furniture, and a sculpture garden. We visited Alessandro Twombly, who treats the palace in Bassano in Teverina—inherited from his father, Cy—as a monumental stage for his own sculptures. Artists' interiors, as we discovered, have a work-in-progress atmosphere that infuses them with a peculiar dynamism.

If artists' homes and studios form the bulk of this volume, we have also included a handful of historical interiors such as Palazzo Leopardi in Recanati, Villa Salviati in Migliarino Pisano, and Palazzo Lanza Tomasi in Palermo, all of which belong to the descendants of the people who created them. They are modern-day custodians who manage, sometimes with great difficulties, to live up to the aesthetic and cultural values that are at the core of these extraordinary interiors. The same desire to pay tribute to the past has inspired Oberto and me to include a handful of museums dedicated to memorable interiors of creative people in the past. These include Casa Mollino in Turin, Museo Mario Praz in Rome, and Museo Filangieri in Naples, a little-known gem in what was once the home of a passionate patron of that city's tradition of arts and crafts.

Italy has long been the land of the world's greatest craftspeople. The tradition continues to this day, which is why Oberto and I have included the rooms of several contemporary craftspeople and designers such as Laura de Santillana, a descendant of the Venini family who continues the Venetian family's tradition of creating works of fine and decorative art in glass. Or Lucia Guarini, who has filled the ancient family place in Scorrano, Puglia, with ceramic artifacts made in her own pottery. Or couturier Stephan Janson's atelier and home in Milan—shared by his partner, Umberto Pasti—pervaded as it is with his taste for dramatic natural and anthropological objects that inspire his creations.

Although "rooms" have been the focus of our attention, we included some of Oberto's cityscapes and landscapes. It may just be a picture of the sea and rocks in Panarea, a view of the Tuscan countryside shot from the car, or a beautiful shot of a piazza or garden in one of the cities. These images, we hope, will help place the interiors in the context of surrounding architecture, geography, or history. Although all the interiors we have chosen are beautiful and somewhat grand, this book is not about luxury. It is about individual talent and the way it shines through and expresses itself in surprising ways in the making, and living, of a room. As well as artists and craftspeople, we have included a few rooms of particularly visionary interior designers, such as Camilla Guinness in Tuscany and the studio of Laura Sartori Rimini and Roberto Peregalli in Milan.

Domus, to conclude, is a totally arbitrary, and therefore incomplete, personal insider's tour into some of the most magnificent, eccentric, and inspiring rooms in Italy today. Oberto Gili and I have imagined this visual "tour" as a contemporary and photographic version of the Grand Tours of the past. Books such as Goethe's *Italian Journey*, Henry James's *Italian Hours*, and Edith Wharton's scholarly words in *Italian Villas and Their Gardens* have been an inspiration. This book, we hope, will bear testimony to the resourcefulness of human creativity in a domestic context and will offer readers a glimpse of the state of the arts and culture in Italy now. We also hope it will inspire them with creative ideas they may want to emulate in their own rooms—and lives.

TURIN IS THE MOST SOLEMN OF ITALIAN CITIES. A BAROQUE JEWEL SET AGAINST A MOUNTAINOUS WILDERNESS. LIKE ALL THINGS MOLDED BY EXTREME RIGOR, IT IS PROFOUNDLY UNPREDICTABLE. VIGOR, LINEARITY, AND STYLE, ITALO CALVINO ONCE CLAIMED, ARE TURIN'S DEFINING QUALITIES, THE PURSUIT OF LOGIC ITS GOAL. AND YET THAT VERY LOGIC, HE ADDED, CAN SOMETIMES LEAD TO MADNESS. NOWHERE IS THIS EXCITING UNPREDICTABILITY MORE TANGIBLE THAN IN ITS ARCHITECTURE. OPPOSITE: THE BAROQUE CUPOLA BY ARCHITECT GUARINO GUARINI IN THE CHURCH OF SAN LORENZO.

CASA MOLLINO

"Anything is allowed," Carlo Mollino wrote, "if it is done with imagination." Mollino was the ultimate Renaissance man, and this apartment the apotheosis of his experimental imagination. It occupies the piano nobile of a late nineteenth-century villa overlooking the Po River in the city where Mollino was born in 1905. The architect—who cultivated a passion for erotic photography, wrote fiction, and was an acrobatic airplane pilot and race-car driver —will be remembered as one of the most influential Italian furniture and interior designers of the twentieth century. These interiors are his philosophical testament to art and design. After buying the apartment incognito in 1960, Mollino gutted the interiors and rebuilt them employing architectural features he designed himself, including Japanese-style sliding doors and a small Louis XV–style mantelpiece. In the living room, pieces of contemporary design were placed against a photographic reproduction of an eighteenth-century German etching. The result is a highly controlled eclecticism. Mollino once described this apartment, which he completed in 1968, as "a warrior's resting place." Interestingly, he never lived here. Nor did he reveal its existence to friends and acquaintances. "He was a true artist," says Fulvio Ferrari, who, with his son Napoleone, acquired the apartment in 1999 and restored it before turning it into a museum by appointment only.

WITH ITS DISTORTED PERSPECTIVES AND ITS LUSCIOUS GARDENS TUCKED AWAY BEHIND STARK WALLS, MILAN—THE CITY OF FASHION AND TASTE PAR EXCELLENCE—NEVER CEASES TO SURPRISE. BEYOND THE FOG AND BENEATH THE SURFACE OF ITS INDUSTRIOUS VENEER, THE FLOWERINGS OF CREATIVITY ARE ENDLESS. OPPOSITE: THE LATE BAROQUE FACADE OF SANTA MARIA DELLA PASSIONE IS ATTRIBUTED TO SCULPTOR GIUSEPPE RUSNATI.

STEPHAN JANSON

"Couturier," an old-fashioned word, is one the French designer Stephan Janson feels most comfortable with. His atelier, ensconced at the back of a verdant courtyard in what used to be a bicycle factory, encapsulates Janson's timeless aesthetic. Clients and visitors are greeted in the entrance hall by a collection of pinned butterflies from Deyrolle, the taxidermy establishment in Paris. "All my objects," he says, "were acquired instinctively. There never was a decorative strategy to fulfill." One such instinctive buy was a large eighteenth-century painted door from a Venetian palazzo. Its presence was something of a burden until Janson built a made-to-measure location for it at the entrance of his showroom. The controlled minimalism of Janson's atelier is complemented by the abundant accumulation of amazing objects, including a collection of tribal headdresses from the Amazon, that defines the interiors of the apartment the couturier shares with his partner, author and gardener Umberto Pasti. "The research for these objects and their haphazard insertion into our everyday environment," says Janson, "have been and continue to be an inspiration."

LAURA SARTORI RIMINI *and* ROBERTO PEREGALLI

Studio Peregalli, the architecture and interior-design firm run by Laura Sartori Rimini and Roberto Peregalli, occupies two separate spaces in two buildings on via Passione, a few steps from the Duomo. The first space, located in an eclectic building from the 1920s, is where their business began some twenty years ago. The second one, just two doors down the road, occupies the ground floor of a nineteenth-century house. For a long time, this second space was used mainly as a deposit for Sartori Rimini's and Peregalli's accumulations of objects and sample materials. Now, after some redecoration, it has been imbued with a lived-in atmosphere that has elevated this space into an extension of their original studio. Each space, says Sartori Rimini, is in harmony with the other and both bear testimony to the studio's philosophy—one that leads them to create made-to-measure interiors for clients all over the world eager to immerse themselves in Studio Peregalli's well-crafted illusions of timelessness. "Reinventing the past as if it were a dream," Sartori Rimini concludes, "makes one appreciate long-lost pleasures and salvaged harmonies."

VENETIAN INTERIORS ARE A COMBINATION OF ARTFULNESS AND NATURE. THE SOARING AMBITION OF ITS ARCHITECTS AND THE EXQUISITE FINESSE OF ITS CRAFTSPEOPLE ARE ELEVATED TO EVEN GREATER HEIGHTS BY THE REFLECTED GLORY OF THE SUN'S RAYS BOUNCING OFF THE WATER TRANSFORMING THE CITY'S ARCHITECTURE AND ITS ROOMS INTO AN OPALESCENT DREAM. OPPOSITE: SANTA MARIA DELLA SALUTE ON VENICE'S PUNTA DELLA DOGANA, IN BETWEEN THE GRAND CANAL AND THE GIUDECCA CANAL.

LAURA DE SANTILLANA

In 1921 Laura de Santillana's grandfather Paolo Venini founded the Venini glass factory on the island of Murano, Venice. "My whole being has been molded by that atmosphere," she says. Vetreria Venini, for which de Santillana worked as a designer for ten years, was sold by her family in 1985. Since then her work has evolved from designing everyday objects to the creation of abstract, sculptural shapes made in blown glass. Her sculptures, which she creates in collaboration with master glassblowers in Venice and abroad, are the protagonists, she says, of her home-studio that occupies a wing in a disused 1890s beer factory on Venice's island of Giudecca. The main room—sixty-five and a half feet (twenty meters) in length by nineteen and a half feet (six meters) in width—is where de Santillana assembles her pieces. The glass theme pervades every inch of the space including a "library" de Santillana designed specifically for her book-shaped glass sculptures. There are no artworks hanging on the walls. The space is sparsely furnished with light, minimalist furniture including modernist-looking chairs designed by Robert Wilson next to the "glass library" and a couple of Harry Bertoia Diamond chairs by Knoll.

PALAZZO PERSICO
VICTORIA PRESS

Born in New York in 1927, Victoria Press created a number of memorable interiors in New York, London, South Africa, again London, and finally Venice, where she died at the age of eighty-eight. A self-taught connoisseur of gardens, architecture, and furniture, she developed a learned passion for Oriental porcelain, putting together a museum-quality collection of blanc de chine, part of which is displayed on white bookshelves she designed for the drawing room on the piano nobile of Palazzo Persico, overlooking the Grand Canal. By the time Press first stepped into it in the mid-1980s, the apartment had been brutally transformed into anonymous offices. Her youngest daughter, Jane da Mosto, an environmental scientist and activist who lives in Venice and who has taken over the apartment since her mother's death, says Press's imagination is what made her see beauty even where it had been banished. She recalls her mother's excitement when, razor blade in hand, she uncovered fragments of original wall decorations buried beneath decades of varnishes. "These decorative elements became her cardinal points," says da Mosto. "They gave her a compass to pursue her own Venetian adventure." The core of this adventure was finding the best craftspeople—wall decorators, cabinetmakers, turners, gesso makers, upholsterers—the city could offer and commissioning them to make furniture and objects Press designed specifically for these interiors.

ROMAMOR

LUIGI ONTANI *and* TULLIA ONTANI

RomAmor is artist Luigi Ontani's architectural folly. This compact villa in the Apennine region was one of several built in the mid-nineteenth century by Cesare Mattei, an eccentric count who lived in a nearby Moorish-style castle and was the pioneer of electrohomeopathy, an obscure alternative medicine. RomAmor was used to host the count's patients who flocked here for his experimental cures. "The architecture of RomAmor featured symbolic and esoteric decorative elements," says Ontani, whose own works are defined by his syncretic use of mythical and religious allegories and symbols. The artist made this place his own through a series of elaborate works of art, both indoors and out, and an extensive use of applied-arts techniques. Hand-painted tiles line walls and floors while ceramic sculptures form prosaic objects such as toilet bowls and tanks. Hanging from the ceiling in every room is a unique chandelier—a "king artichoke" in the dining room, "the hummingbird's shiver" in the tearoom— each designed by Ontani and produced in Murano. His quest for total design encompasses every detail of RomAmor including furniture. Across the garden and below an intricate labyrinth—designed by the artist and tended to by Tullia, his green-thumbed sister—is Ontani's studio displaying a flourish of decorative elements including a mosaic representation of the four seasons on the facade. "In RomAmor," Ontani ponders, "art climbed out of the painting to frame life itself."

CARRARA'S MOTTO—"MY FORCE IS IN THE WHEEL"—IS ROOTED IN ITS LEGENDARY QUAR-
RIES. FOR OVER TWO THOUSAND YEARS THIS MOUNTAINOUS REGION IN NORTHWEST TUSCANY,
POPULATED BY A COMMUNITY OF RADICAL THINKERS THAT GAVE RISE TO ONE OF THE FIRST
ANARCHIC MOVEMENTS IN EUROPE, HAS BEEN PROVIDING THE FINEST MARBLE TO ARTISTS AND
ARCHITECTS FOR THEIR SCULPTURES, TEMPLES, PALACES, AND CHURCHES. THIS IS THE ORI-
GIN OF SOME OF THE GREATEST MASTERPIECES IN THE HISTORY OF WESTERN ART. OPPOSITE: A
MARBLE QUARRY IN CARRARA.

NICOLI FAMILY

In the nineteenth century there were over one hundred marble-carving workshops in the city of Carrara that were run by as many families, all of whom gave work to thousands of specialized craftsmen. Nowadays there are fewer than a dozen. The Carlo Nicoli workshop, one of the most prominent since the region's heyday, is a rare survivor of this ancient craft. Founded in 1835 by a sculptor who named the workshop after himself, it is now run by a namesake descendant and his daughter, Francesca Nicoli. In the course of two centuries, craftsmen of the Carlo Nicoli workshop have worked on sculptures commissioned by governments, institutions, and individual artists all over the world. The current owners inhabit the house built by the founder, situated next to the workshop. It is a mid-nineteenth-century neo-Gothic throwback filled with books, family portraits, and marble artifacts that bear testimony to eight generations and nearly two centuries dedicated to this quintessentially Italian craft.

PERCHED ON THE EDGE OF A VAST STRETCH OF UNTAMED FOREST AND COASTLINE, THE TINY TOWN OF MIGLIARINO PISANO IS THE IDEAL STARTING POINT TO EXPLORE THE PARK OF MIGLIARINO, SAN ROSSORE, A DREAM COME TRUE FOR NATURALISTS, ORNITHOLOGISTS, AND BOTANISTS. WITH ITS MARBLE-LINED CATHEDRAL AND ITS ICONIC LEANING TOWER, PISA'S PIAZZA DEI MIRACOLI—A SHORT DRIVE SOUTHEAST FROM HERE—IS ONE OF ITALY'S FINEST ARCHITECTURAL COMPLEXES. OPPOSITE: PISA'S LEANING TOWER.

VILLA SALVIATI

SALVIATI FAMILY

Of all the great Tuscan villas, Villa Salviati, just off the coast south of Pisa, is the most eccentric. Immersed in a vast and magnificent property of woods and farmland, this villa was built in the 1860s by an Alsatian architect, Joseph-Antoine Froelicher, for Duke Scipione Salviati, an influential Catholic politician who had strenuously sided with Pope Pius IX against the newborn Italian state and the decision to make Rome the nation's capital. After the pope's defeat and his retreat to the Vatican state in 1870, Scipione Salviati and his wife, Arabella Fitz James, made their base in Migliarino. The duke drained the marshland, an epic feat at the time. He built a church, a school, and housing for the many families of workers on his property. As for the villa, Scipione and his wife opted for the ornate style in vogue in France at the time. Flowery French cottons were imported from the venerable Braquenié in Paris to upholster walls and furniture, some of which, like many pieces in the dining and living rooms, were made to measure. In the last few years Grazia Salviati, the current duchess, asked Federico Forquet, the great couturier turned interior designer, to help her and her husband, Forese, restore these interiors to their original splendor.

FLORENCE. THE NAME ITSELF—FROM THE LATIN *FLORENTIA*—CONJURES IMAGES OF FLOW-
ERS AND BLOSSOMS. IF GARDENS COULD BE MADE OF MARBLE AND STONE, FLORENCE WOULD
BE THEIR APOTHEOSIS. THIS CITY NURTURED, WITHIN ITS FOLDS, THE GREATEST AND MOST
ENDURING FLOWERING IN THE WESTERN WORLD: THE RENAISSANCE. OPPOSITE: A FACADE OF
SANTA MARIA DEL FIORE, KNOWN MORE COMMONLY AS THE DUOMO.

FIONA CORSINI *and*
DIEGO DI SAN GIULIANO

It took seven years for Fiona Corsini and Diego di San Giuliano to transform this rural hamlet on the peak of via San Leonardo, overlooking Florence, into a home. "The result is a collaboration amongst a group of like-minded friends, including architect Themistocle Antoniadis, painter Alex Hamilton, and Oliva di Collobiano for the garden," says painter Corsini, who made the luminous panels in the dining room. Interiors and exteriors are interchangeable, with meals often taken outdoors and plants growing indoors. "Many curious-looking and unpredictable corners I have created for the sole purpose of painting them," says Corsini, who completed her studies at the Florence Academy of Art. Most of the materials used, including the marble Art Deco mantelpiece in the living room and the early twentieth-century floor tiles, were salvaged during trips to remote areas of Italy. Other pieces, such as the library and the long wooden banquette in the living room, were made to measure. The walls were hand-painted by Corsini and her friends Caterina Enni Misson and Francesca Guicciardini. This road is famous for having been the address of many creative people. Ottone Rosai, the painter, had his studio on this same property, and Pyotr Ilyich Tchaikovsky lived a few doors down. "This history inspired me to rely on my instincts and my imagination," says Corsini, "rather than on tradition."

PALAZZO CAPPONI CANIGIANI
SUE TOWNSEND

Palazzo Capponi Canigiani is one of the jewels of Florentine private architecture. So much so that—as a marble plaque on the palazzo's facade informs—Sir John Pope-Hennessy, the British scholar of Renaissance art, lived here for decades until his death in 1994. "When I took over the apartment, there were still signs of his presence, such as his library," says Sue Townsend, a British-born entrepreneur who came to live in Florence in the early 2000s, where she founded Ortigia, a brand of soaps and fragrances based on Sicilian essences. "I took everything out in order to fit my own things." Judging from Townsend's vast collection of eighteenth- and early nineteenth-century English, Irish, French, and Italian furniture and paintings, this was no easy feat. Townsend commissioned artistic friends to *make* things, including the dozens of painted portraits of her dogs, past and present, in the kitchen. Another commission is in her oval-shaped dining room, which Alex Hamilton painted with classically inspired architectural themes. "I love having things made: tables, lamps, and even fabric." What gives a unique character to these interiors is Townsend's unabashed Britishness. Both the living room and the library, filled with her eclectic assortment of furniture, books, and objets d'art, pay tribute to the legacy of early twentieth-century Anglo-American expatriates who transformed Florentine villas and palaces into living museums.

VILLA LE CORTI
OLIVA DI COLLOBIANO

Gardener, watercolorist, and writer Oliva di Collobiano lives at Villa Le Corti, the Renaissance estate belonging to the princely Corsini family to whom she is related. She occupies what used to be the farmer's home overlooking a landscape of vineyards and olive groves. One of her favorite places is the villa's "precious" garden. Enclosed by an ancient wall, it is an intimate version of the classic Italian garden, with topiary box hedges punctuated here and there by persimmon and apple trees. "My task at the villa," says di Collobiano, who studied art at the academy in Turin before turning her attention to the world of plants, "has been to clean out the area of the garden from redundancies." In the course of decades creating or restoring some of Italy's best-loved gardens, di Collobiano has developed an awareness of the delicate balance between the garden and the landscape. She is not interested in exotic extravagances and was one of the first in Italy to plant wild flowers and humble, local plants inside the garden. What she has brought into her home, from her experience on the "field," is the pleasure of keeping things simple. "I tend to my home in the same way I do a comforting, familiar landscape," di Collobiano concludes. "Harmonious order always allows for a certain degree of natural spontaneity."

AVANE

MATTHEW SPENDER
and MARO GORKY

In the forty or so years since they took over Avane, sculptor Matthew Spender and painter Maro Gorky have transformed their 1750 Tuscan farmhouse into an extraordinary artistic feat.

"Artists are people who make things with their own hands, so there's continuity between our lives and those who have lived here over the previous centuries. Instead of hoes and mattocks, there are hammers and chisels and blocks of stone—but the hoes are also still here, as we keep a large kitchen garden. Every room in the house has a handmade quality that is an extension of the works we make in other materials. Several of the rooms are frescoed by Maro, so that what she paints on paper or canvas has now extended to the walls. Built-in bookshelves and wooden cupboards have been carved by me. It's a 'total house.' There's no gap between the building and the people who live in it. We've never taken the advice of an architect, and the idea that most people hand over their apartments and houses to those who make straight lines on paper seems, to us, crazy. Why delegate one of the great joys of life, which is to make yours the place where you live?" —Matthew Spender

CASTELLO DI POTENTINO

GRAHAM *and* SALLY GREENE, ALEXANDER GREENE, *and* CHARLOTTE HORTON

"Traditions that give identity are being progressively eroded, even in Italy," says Charlotte Horton, who lives and works at Castello di Potentino with her brother, Alexander Greene, and their mother, Sally. They found that in this relatively poor rural area off the maps of mass tourism, local customs and practices had survived. "When my family discovered Potentino in 1999, it was like stepping onto the set of Jean Cocteau's *Beauty and the Beast*," Horton recalls. "We scrabbled up and over a ruined wall and tumbled into a magical courtyard overgrown with roses." Horton and the Greenes have been restoring the castle ever since. They have also been playing a role in preserving the cultural identity of Monte Amiata. "The castle, in its heyday, represented a continuation of the archaic relationship between man and his environment," Horton continues. "I feel it should continue to play its role as dynamic cultural hub." If wine and olive oil are the main produce of Castello di Potentino, what keeps the place bustling are the projects that revolve around it: art shows, concerts, and a line of furniture and objects for the home devised with designer Nigel Coates and made with locally sourced materials and produced under the name of #paracastello. "Potentino," Horton concludes, "is a philosophy of life: one that is imbued with humanistic values."

CASTELLO ROMITORIO
SANDRO CHIA

Artist and wine producer Sandro Chia divides his time between the United States and his property near Montalcino, Tuscany.

"The shape of the sixteenth-century Castello Romitorio is anamorphic; thanks to its four towers placed at slanting angles around a central rectangle, it eludes a systematic vision of its perimeter. The walls, at their base, measure two meters [six and a half feet] in depth. The windows, relatively small and high above ground level, are difficult to access from outside. It is the ideal place for a solitary spirit. The name itself, Romitorio, is an allusion to the hermits who from the sixth century onwards chose this hill as their refuge. The first time I heard about it was from Giorgio Franchetti, an intellectual who befriended artists and was something of a mentor to me. He had decided this was the place for me. I was living in New York so I didn't take him up on it. Five years later, on the phone, I asked him what happened to the castle. He said: 'It's waiting for you.' I flew to Rome the next day and drove up to Tuscany. I knew it was going to be mine before I reached the destination. I was answering a call from destiny. To mix my life with those old stones, to make myself at home amongst them, has been and continues to be an interesting experience."
—Sandro Chia

ARNIANO

CAMILLA GUINNESS

Camilla Guinness and her late husband, Jasper, bought Arniano, a farmhouse on a hill near Montalcino, in 1989. It had walls, ceilings, windows, and little else—not even running water or electricity. "What surprised us was how light and airy these interiors felt compared to most Tuscan farmhouses," Guinness recalls. She scoured the area for inspiration. The design for the white mantelpiece in the living room is a copy of one she saw at Cetinale, one of the great Renaissance villas in Tuscany. "Making these interiors opened my eyes to the versatility and genius of Italian craftspeople," she says. Guinness, who is an interior designer, designed many of the objects in the house—tables, beds, lamps, cupboards—and had them made by local ironmongers and cabinetmakers. With the help of Tuscan builders she transformed the archaic architectural features, such as the original mangers for the animals into seating areas. Artist friends were encouraged to contribute their talents to the decoration. The painted wall decorations in one of the bedrooms, with a stylized version of the trees and landscape surrounding the house, is the fruit of one of many such collaborations. "This house is where I first began to play with rooms," says Guinness. Like these rooms, a perfect mix of English style and Italian crafts, Arniano's garden—planted in the course of many years by Jasper Guinness—is an English gardener's tribute to local aromatic plants.

DOMITILLA HARDING

Artist and designer of furniture and interiors, Domitilla Harding divides her time between London and this remote property in the hills of southern Tuscany.

"In 1981 I was happily lost exploring the magnificent woods that surround Siena when I came upon this hamlet. It took my breath away to discover such an unspoiled dream from the past, completely overgrown—a time capsule abandoned by its owners and inhabited by a lonely hermit who thought Italy was still at war. Maybe he was the last survivor of what had been during that time a hidden partisan headquarters. It was love at first sight and two years later I purchased it from a family of thirty who had run it as their farm since 1500. They had lived on the upper floors above the cattle, pigs, goats, and chickens, and in time they had decorated their rooms with layers and layers of stenciling. I am still fascinated by the lives whose presence still pervades these rooms. For decades we lived off grid without electricity or a telephone. Luckily water was found twenty meters [sixty-five and a half feet] underground. The difficulties made life necessarily simple. This remote place with limited access to materials and resources has influenced my work as an artist and designer of glass sculptures and objects. When I am in the city, where everything is available, I long for the modesty of this place." —Domitilla Harding

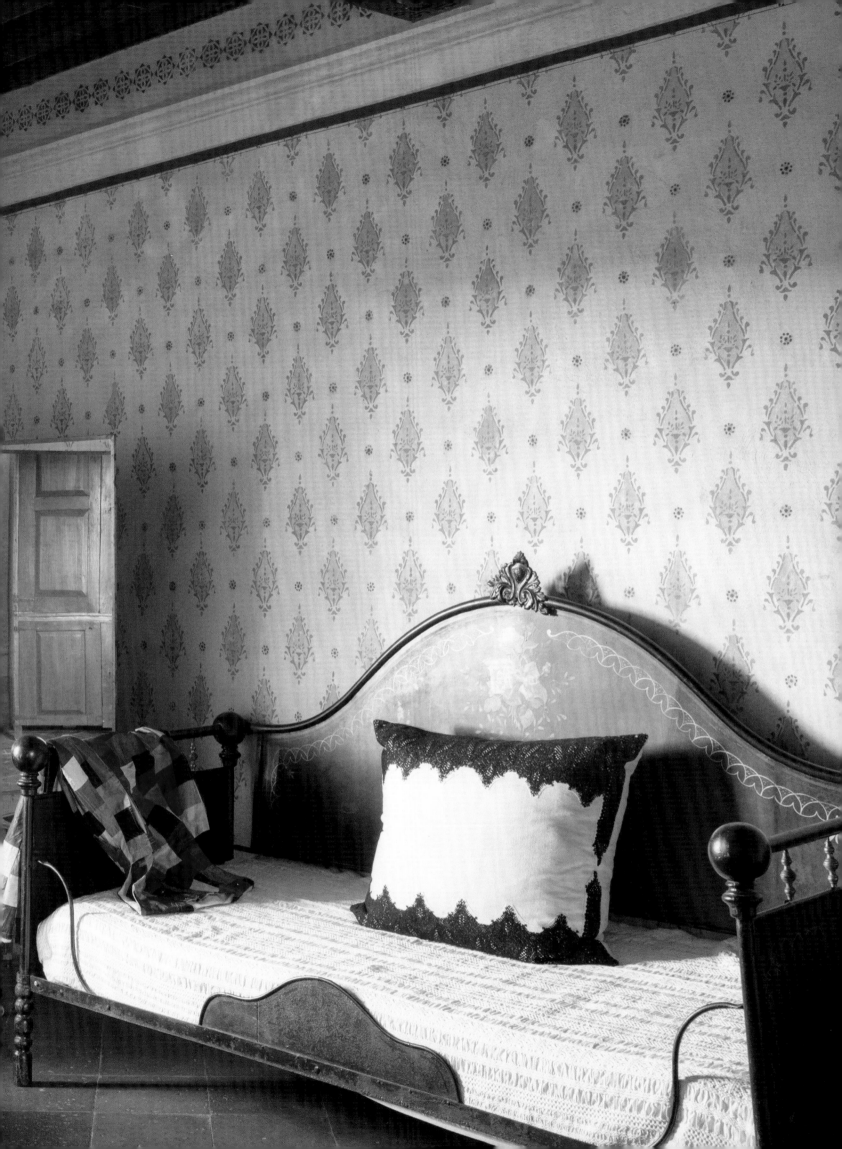

CONVENTO DI SANTA CROCE
EMILY YOUNG

"I needed a place that could support the presence of my sculptures," Emily Young says of her move from London to the Convento di Santa Croce in Tuscany. Built in 1620 and immersed in a landscape of olive groves and Mediterranean shrubs, the convent had long belonged to Adam Pollock, a close friend of Young's, who had used it as a monumental stage set for his Batignano Opera Festival. With its cloister and its roofless church, it was the ideal setting for Young's larger-than-life sculptures in marble and stone. "The work I do here is about being connected to the earth and respecting her," she says. Some of Young's sculptures have been placed in an opening between the olive groves and the forest. This is her tribute to the classic Italian tradition of sculpture gardens. "I want the convent to be alive, but quiet. This was a sacred space, built as a sacred space, and I want to keep that feeling." Whitewashed, vaulted rooms on the ground floor are sparsely furnished. The artist lives here all year round, often in the company of assistants, friends, or family members; yet, the Convento di Santa Croce does not feel like a home. "I don't want it to become a big comfortable place with amazing sofas everywhere," Young says. "One sofa, for that place to go and crash at the end of the day, is more than enough."

IL CAMPO
GIOVANNI SANJUST DI TEULADA

Artist Giovanni Sanjust di Teulada lived in a small trailer parked to one end of Il Campo, his nearly thirty-acre (twelve-hectare) property in southern Tuscany. Despite his quest for a life of Rousseauian simplicity, he spent the last two decades of his life single-handedly transforming this flat, empty field between the railway tracks and the Tyrrhenian coast into his very own Shangri-la. Il Campo's classically inspired villa, which the artist built and decorated himself, overlooks a garden of delights with rosebushes and rare irises, olive groves, cypress trees, and a vast labyrinth of topiary oak hedges. Inhabiting this dreamy landscape are families of wild boar, buffaloes, horses, and hundreds of the most decorative species of chicken—including giant Brahmas and graceful Sumatras—that Sanjust could find. These animals are often the protagonists of the artist's painted landscapes and of his sculptures. "Once upon a time there used to be Ligabue, the painter-peasant," Sanjust once commented. "I am a painter-farmer." The artist died in October 2014, at sixty-one, crushed by his tractor while tending to his garden.

IL GIARDINO DEI TAROCCHI
NIKI DE SAINT PHALLE

When artist Niki de Saint Phalle first appeared at the Caracciolo brothers' home in southern Tuscany in 1977, she was holding a clay model of what was to become one of the greatest sculpture gardens of the twentieth century: the Tarot Garden. One of the first things de Saint Phalle built was a huge empress figure in the shape of a sphinx. The cavernous interiors became the artist's home in Garavicchio for two decades. Her bedroom was in one breast, the kitchen in another, and the entrance was via an arched portal in between the creature's massive buttocks. There were no straight lines in de Saint Phalle's home environment. The windows were round and the walls and ceiling looked as if they had been molded in soft clay. The shower was in the shape of a benign-looking anaconda with water spurting from its fangs. In time, the whitewashed walls and the kitchen appliances were covered with a mosaic of hand-cut mirrors that heightened the dreamlike power of the artist's fantasy world. From the sphinx, de Saint Phalle would impart instructions to her team of builders, plumbers, ceramicists, and mosaicists. In winter evenings, a fire would be lit in its belly and dinner would be served. Hanging above her dining table, also covered in mosaic, is a sculpture by Jean Tinguely, one of many in the garden that bear testimony to his presence in de Saint Phalle's life.

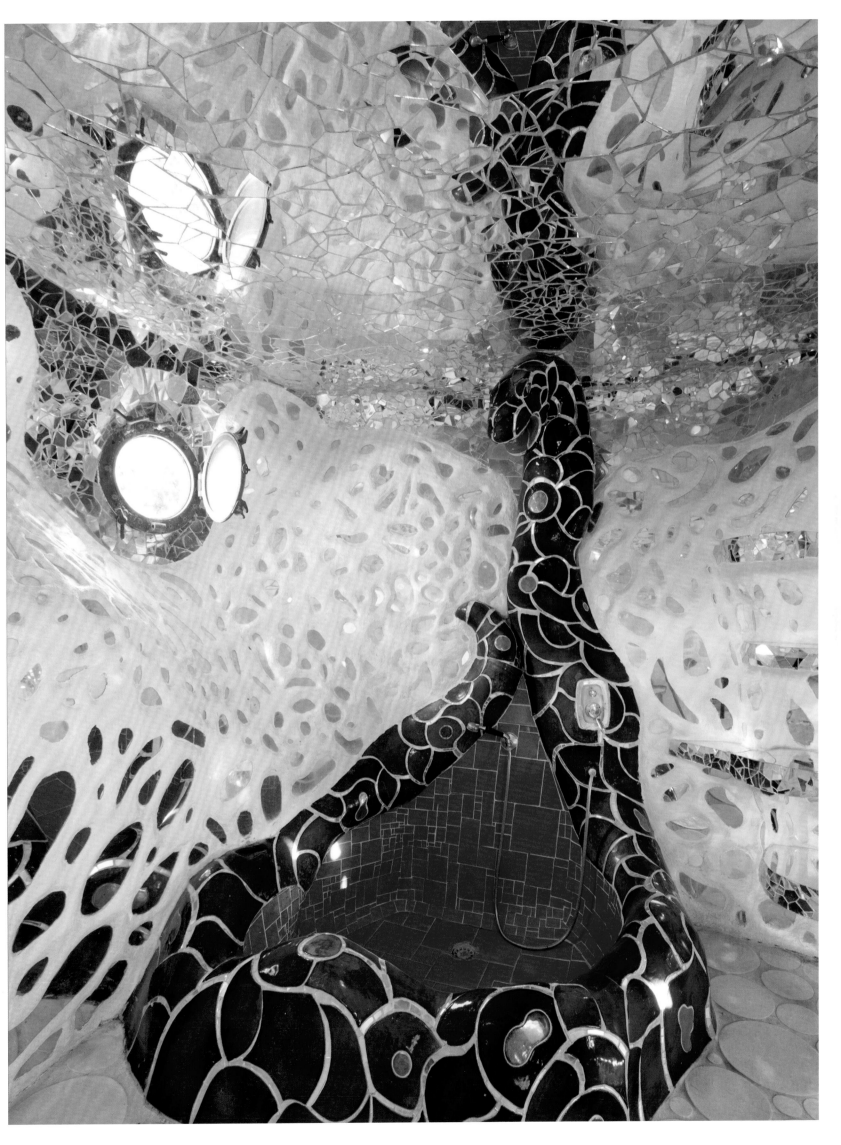

TRISTANO DI ROBILANT

Tristano di Robilant makes sculptures out of glass and ceramics: solemn, sensuous shapes that reflect or filter their surroundings. So when the artist decided to leave his studio in the center of Rome and move to quieter surroundings, light was his main objective. He found what he was looking for in a semi-abandoned 1920s ceramic factory in Ripabianca, a tiny village of some five hundred inhabitants surrounded by a forested landscape. "In certain hours of the day," he says, "the light in these rooms is almost palpable." In these sparsely furnished interiors, di Robilant has applied his art to a domestic use with a series of painted plates, tiles, and lamps made out of glass or terra-cotta.

LEOPARDI FAMILY

Poet Giacomo Leopardi was born in 1798 in his family's eighteenth-century palazzo in the town of Recanati. The entire first floor of the palace houses the family library. Assembled by Monaldo Leopardi—whose son, the poet, described as a man "excessively jealous of his books"—this extraordinary collection consists of more than twenty thousand volumes on theology, engineering, ophthalmology, economics, mathematics, astrology, travel, and other subjects. Many of its volumes—including works by Montesquieu, Rousseau, Voltaire, Diderot, d'Alembert, Chateaubriand, de Staël, and Goethe—are first editions. The Manuscripts Room contains a number of early works by Giacomo Leopardi. First opened to the public by Monaldo Leopardi in 1812, the library—and a small museum next to it—is tended to by Count Vanni and Olimpia Leopardi, a father-and-daughter team who inhabit the top floors of the palace. "We are the custodians of a valuable legacy," says Olimpia, "and we are doing all in our power to ensure it will be passed down to the generations to come."

TWOMBLY STUDIO

This seventeenth-century palazzo sits on an outcrop of tufa overlooking the Tiber River valley north of Rome. When artist Cy Twombly discovered it in the early 1970s, the palace and the tiny village surrounding it were in a state of semi-abandonment. Twombly—with the help of his brother-in-law Giorgio Franchetti, an art collector and expert in philological restorations of ancient buildings—restored the palazzo, creating an inner courtyard. Twombly relished Bassano in Teverina's remoteness and its centuries-old patina. He lived and worked here during the summer for thirty years, until his death in 2011. It now belongs to his son, Alessandro, who uses it as a gallery for his own sculptures.

CAIOLO

ALESSANDRO TWOMBLY

Sculptor and painter Alessandro Twombly is based in Italy, where his father, Cy, came to live in the late 1950s. Alessandro's mother was the Italian artist Tatiana Franchetti. The artist is also a botanist and collector of rare plants.

"Caiolo—that's the name of my house—stands on the slopes overlooking the lake of Vico in the province of Viterbo, also known as Tuscia. The numerous lakes in this region are water fill-ups of volcanic craters that became inactive some nine million years ago. Built in the early nineteenth century as a *casale*, a local word that indicates the landlord's residence on a farming estate, Caiolo was restored in the 1990s: large, arched window-doors were opened around the square perimeter of the building in order to let more sunlight in and create a connection with the surrounding garden. The ground floor is a large open space. Upstairs are four simple rooms with decorated coffered ceilings. A large greenhouse room was added to the original structure as an extra living space in the warmer months. The farm produces hazelnuts and olive oil, while the garden hosts a collection of oak species from all around the world and a sizeable number of ancient roses." —Alessandro Twombly

VILLA LINA
PAOLA IGLIORI

Originally built in the 1920s on the remains of an eighteenth-century villa and botanical park in the town of Ronciglione, Villa Lina consists of several buildings, most of them rural, immersed in a vast, elaborate garden designed in the 1930s by architect Raffaele de Vico. The estate belongs to Paola Igliori—writer, filmmaker, and organic farmer. Of all the buildings she could have lived in—including a villa filled with works by artists who lived in New York in the 1980s and 1990s—she chose the most humble: an old pigsty. Igliori proclaims, "Making an interior beautiful is a question of taste and imagination." And of color. Like the red on white hand-painted motifs—inspired by ancient Mediterranean cultures—used to decorate walls and ceilings and some of the furniture, too. "That's really all it took," says Igliori, "to transform three sheds, one for each pig, and a horse stable into my very own miniature palace."

PALAZZO PATRIZI

RANIERO GNOLI

This seventeenth-century castle nestled in the rugged woodlands of the Tuscia region north of Rome looks nothing like it did in the early 1960s when Count Raniero Gnoli, a renowned scholar of Tantric Buddhism and one of the world's experts in Roman and Byzantine marble, first came to see it. The castle was stunning but crumbling, having been vacated for a century. "There were hundreds of hens living in these rooms," recalls Gnoli, who took over the second floor. "It was a colossal chicken coop." Wielding paint and brushes, Gnoli marbleized the ceilings and brushed on yards of trompe l'oeil wainscot. Watercolors depicting flowers and animals, such as a series of allegorical monkeys inspired by the writings of Erasmus, are Gnoli's work too. He is handy with needle and thread and fashioned the beds' ornate canopies. His travels across India were the source for the cottons and raw silks curtaining the apartment's tall windows. These do-it-yourself projects reach an apotheosis in a vaulted chamber Gnoli describes as the Wunderkammer. In this room of wonders, a gigantic egg from a long-extinct ostrich from Madagascar dangles from a beam, and African turtle shells, narwhal tusks, and fossils compete for attention with cabinets, tables, and pedestals laden with seashells and rock crystal. His latest task, as yet incomplete, is a monumental globe that awaits its painted continents and oceans.

BRUNO AMMANN
and MYUNGSOOK JEON

The home of mosaicist Bruno Ammann and of his wife, Myungsook Jeon, is surrounded by a forest outside the town of Sacrofano, north of Rome. One reaches it via a dirt road winding its way through the woodland. "We bought this plot of land in 1985," says Ammann in a French accent that reveals his origins, "and the first year we camped out in a hut that had a roof and three walls." The fourth he made using slabs of wood lined with newspapers to keep the cold out. The rest of the house he built with his own hands, progressively, one room at a time to make space for a growing family. Ammann's artistic career began in Paris in the 1960s when he worked for Lino Melano, the mosaicist from Ravenna who collaborated with some of the great artists of his time. "Thanks to him," Ammann recalls, "I worked with Braque and Chagall, amongst others." These interiors—sober, unassuming, sparsely furnished—pay tribute to some of the artists Ammann worked with. On one wall, next to a wicker chair, is a mosaic inspired by a painting by Alberto Magnelli. On another, next to the piano, is a piece inspired by the Franco-Algerian artist Jean-Michel Attlan, while the bathroom is dominated by a mosaic commissioned by Giulio Turcato, one of the members of the Italian abstract informal art movement.

WHETHER THEY LIVE IN PRINCELY PALAZZOS OR MORE MODEST ABODES, MODERN-DAY ROMANS CANNOT ESCAPE PAYING SOME SORT OF TRIBUTE, SOMETIMES SUFFUSED WITH IRONY, TO THEIR CITY'S PAST. THIS IS AFTER ALL, AS NOVELIST GEORGE ELIOT ONCE NOTED, "THE CITY OF VISIBLE HISTORY." ROMA CAPUT MUNDI: THE CAPITAL OF THE WORLD. OPPOSITE: SCULPTURES OF ATHLETES AT THE FORO ITALICO (ORIGINALLY CALLED THE FORO MUSSOLINI), THE SPORTING COMPLEX COMMISSIONED BY BENITO MUSSOLINI AND COMPLETED IN 1938.

MILTON GENDEL

"Oh, you're in Rome? Come for a drink!" Milton Gendel must have uttered this invitation thousands of times in the last sixty-five or so years during which he has made himself at home in a remarkable succession of Roman interiors. And every time it is music to the ears of those passing through the Eternal City or who simply want to touch base with this multi-talented American—art historian, photographer, diarist, journalist, war veteran, collector, and indomitable raconteur—and breathe in, glass in hand, that cosmopolitan mix of pre–Second World War New York art scene, *dolce vita* ease, and old-world *Wunderkammer* eccentricity. Gendel, a close associate of the Surrealists who had regrouped to New York in the 1930s, arrived in Rome in 1949 on a Fulbright scholarship. One of the attractions of Rome at the time, he says, was the possibility of living in splendid interiors. "Rome in the 1950s and '60s was an outpost of the New York art world," he says. His interiors are decorated with furniture and some old-master paintings Gendel salvaged from Porta Portese, the Roman flea market he has been visiting nearly every Sunday, at the crack of dawn, for over sixty-five years. When asked what makes a good interior, he is elusive. "What you need is for your soul to feel happy in it," he says.

ORSINA SFORZA

When painter Orsina Sforza began to make lamps out of recycled household materials she did so, she says, out of necessity: "Light is the defining element in any room." In the daytime Sforza's residence, which she shares with her film producer husband, and her studio on the top two floors of a 1930s building in the ancient quarter of San Saba are an ode to sunlight. For light after dark, however, she had to rely on her own devices. "The first rule is to have as many sources of illumination as possible," she says. In her living room she has fifteen. The second rule is that some of these sources of light must be white, for reading, while others should emanate a suffused, tinted light, which gives depth to a room. Many of Sforza's early lights were made with hand-painted parchment placed on unusual stands, often abandoned objects she found outdoors during her daily walks. In time, these lamps have evolved into proper sculptures made with a variety of materials: recycled pastry papers and coffee filters, lightly crushed and pieced together to create large cloudlike shapes, or household fabric, such as napkins and tea towels, dropped in liquid starch and molded to take on dynamic shapes akin to Bernini's drape-like effects.

ROMOLO BULLA
and ROSALBA BULLA

A stone's throw from Piazza del Popolo, the focal point of Rome's thriving artistic community right through the 1970s, is Litografia R. Bulla, the city's great printing workshop for artists. Romolo and Rosalba Bulla, brother and sister, are the current generation of a time-honored dynasty of lithographers and printers—one that originated in northern Italy before moving to France, where forebears opened their first print shop in 1814, and, after finally settling in Rome, where they established a lithography studio in 1840. "At the end of each working day our father used to open a couple of wine bottles in the entrance hall," Romolo Bulla recalls, "and our studio would become a salon in which ideas on art would be fervently discussed." Romolo and Rosalba were children when Giorgio de Chirico, André Masson, and most of the great Italian artists of the twentieth century came here to work side by side with their father. Other artists, including Cy Twombly and Jim Dine, followed suit. "These interiors may look like a time warp," says Rosalba, "but that's because every surface bears the traces of a long and intense history in printing and lithography."

PALAZZO MASSIMO LANCELLOTTI
CORALLA MAIURI

Coralla Maiuri's studio occupies a handful of rooms on the top floor of the sixteenth-century palace that belongs to the family of her husband, Prince Filippo Massimo Lancellotti. The baroque atmosphere that pervades most of the palace's overwrought interiors dissolves as soon as one steps into Maiuri's ethereal, light-filled quarters. An inspiring interior, the artist suggests, is one unburdened by sentimental or historic connotations. Objects should be sparse, and the placement of furniture dictated by necessity rather than aesthetics. "This is a world unto itself," reflects Maiuri.

ISABELLA DUCROT

Artist and fabric collector Isabella Ducrot was born in Naples and lives between Rome and Umbria, where—with her husband, Vicky Ducrot, an Indian-miniatures expert—they have planted a garden of rare roses.

"I have lived on the third floor of this Roman palazzo for years and from my terrace I can look into the hushed courtyard below. A handful of rooms off the courtyard used to be inhabited by a monsignor. Sometimes I would catch myself peering into his large window. There was a red curtain and, beyond it, a table filled with books. In the evening, when the monsignor returned home from the Vatican, he would turn on the lights and I could glimpse his solemn figure sitting at the table, writing. Those mysterious rooms, and their even more mysterious inhabitant, were a source of fascination for me. Little did I know that one day I myself would occupy those same rooms. Having been promoted to a higher position within the Vatican hierarchy, the high prelate vacated the apartment. Soon after, I moved in with my working tables, my canvases, and my colors. It became my studio. These two spaces are still deeply connected in my mind. The home on the third floor is where I live with my husband, Vicky, and where many of our daily activities take place. My studio off the courtyard is where I allow my imagination to roam freely." —Isabella Ducrot

PALAZZO PRIMOLI

MUSEO MARIO PRAZ

"What is a home but a projection of the self?" As a consequence of his dictum, Mario Praz, the Anglicist and author of the seminal volume *An Illustrated History of Interior Decoration* (1964), experienced decoration as an indirect way to cultivate his own inner self. Judging from Praz's apartment—filled as it is with exquisite neoclassical objets d'art, paintings, and furniture collected during a lifetime—his preferred way to express his "self" was through monothematic accumulations. His collection is one of the lesser-known glories of modern Rome. It is also the subject of Praz's autobiography, *The House of Life*. Since his death in 1982, the interiors of Praz's last Roman residence, which occupy part of the second floor of Palazzo Primoli, overlooking the Tiber, have been turned into a museum.

JULIE POLIDORO

Color is the defining element in Julie Polidoro's work. The artist applies pure powder pigments on vast, loosely hung canvases, leaving large areas of them uncovered so as to reveal the rough texture of the fabric. "I do the same thing in my living quarters," she says. "At home, I deliberately leave some areas in every room unencumbered: quiet, colorless spaces in which my vision can roam freely." Her compact two-bedroom apartment in the Trastevere neighborhood, a few steps from the eighteenth-century botanical gardens, is a mathematical exercise in controlled minimalism. "I actually count the amount of objects I live with. For all new pieces that come in, I make sure the same amount, of the same proportions, goes out," says the artist. Most of the pieces of furniture in her home are family heirlooms that she has covered with brightly colored upholstery or paint. Another familiar touch is in the geometric fabrics, hand-painted by her sister Zazie Gnecchi Ruscone, that cover the cushions.

ANTONIO MONFREDA

Rome-based art director Antonio Monfreda is one of founders of The Visual Clinic, a multimedia lab for video and photo productions.

"I tend to live in small spaces so I can control every detail of my living environment. Symmetry is an essential element for me, which is why the objects I prefer tend to come in pairs. When I can't find the pair I am looking for, I design them myself and have them made, like the cube-shaped tables in the main room—each one with an incorporated lamp. I designed them with Patrick Kinmonth, the opera director and stage designer. Aside from a large carved-wood 'armoire,' where my grandmother used to store biscuits and teacakes, there is little space in these rooms for nostalgia. Making a home is very much like editing one's own life. Objects come and go or change position as one evolves. Whether I am staging an exhibition or planning a room, space—and not objects—is ultimately what determines the outcome."
—Antonio Monfreda

NAPLES, CALLED *NOVAPOLIS* BY THE EARLY ROMANS. ONE OF THE OLDEST "NEW CITIES" IN THE WORLD. LAYERED, RICH, AND STRANGE. A PLACE WHERE PAST AND PRESENT MERGE IN A CONTINUOUS STRUGGLE. MAGNIFICENTLY ALOOF AND ABSOLUTELY CONTEMPORARY. IT IS THE CITY OF THE TWENTY-FIRST CENTURY. OPPOSITE: CASTEL DELL'OVO ON THE GULF OF NAPLES.

PALAZZO COMO

MUSEO CIVICO
GAETANO FILANGIERI

The Filangieri is a gem of a museum. Situated on the via Duomo in the center of Naples, these little-known interiors, which first opened to the public in 1888, offer a total immersion into the grandiose eclecticism that inspired the Italian Arts and Crafts movement during the late nineteenth century. Founded in 1882 by an enlightened Neapolitan—Gaetano Filangieri, Prince of Satriano—the museum occupies two floors of the fifteenth-century Palazzo Como, also known as "the palace that walks," because in the 1880s the entire building had to be moved back some sixty-five and a half feet (twenty meters) in order to make space for the new via Duomo. The museum—which owes much of its existence to the support of an association of Neapolitan intellectuals (www.salviamoilmuseofilangieri.org)—hosts Gaetano Filangieri's ancient arms collection as well as his artistic accumulations: paintings and sculptures, pottery and ceramics. Collections aside, what makes this museum unique is its neo-Gothic interiors in which every detail, from the hand-painted majolica floors and the carved ceiling decorations to the elaborate boiseries and spiral staircase leading to the library, contributes to the overall design narrative.

MICHELE IODICE

Artist Michele Iodice's studio occupies a grotto inside an ancient tufa quarry in Naples. Access to it is via an opening squeezed between two palazzos on the road leading up the mountain to the Museo Capodimonte—a former royal palace and, since 1957, an important museum. This archaic interior, one of many that were hand-carved directly into the stone mountain on which the museum stands, has served at different times as a stable, a warehouse, and a refuge for the local population during Second World War air raids over Naples. "What makes this grotto unusual is the amount of natural light that enters into it," notes the artist. The space is filled with Iodice's surreal artistic installations evoking mythical symbols and shapes from a distant past. In time, this grotto has evolved from serving as a theatrical setting for Iodice's works into an artwork itself.

FIORE MONFREDA FABIANI

She could have chosen the largest and grandest house on Panarea. Instead the late
Fiore Monfreda Fabiani went for the tiniest and most humble of them all—a *"pied
dans l'eau"* cubicle that looks like a boat. Four rooms and an open-air loggia take in
one of the most mythical views of the Mediterranean: Dattilo, Basiluzzo, and the volcanic island of Stromboli, in the Aeolian Islands. This is a house made of nothing
much except sunshine and a view. The whitewashed walls, with turquoise finishes
around doorways and windows, provide the ideal background for a small collection
of colorfully painted wooden artifacts and ceramics from Sicily, which she would
often fill with citrus from the garden. Furniture is solely functional. Necessities, the
only luxury. Nothing to distract from the ultimate role of a room or, indeed, a house:
that of making one feel connected to the landscape.

TO HAVE SEEN ITALY WITHOUT HAVING SEEN SICILY, JOHANN WOLFGANG VON GOETHE WROTE, IS NOT TO HAVE SEEN ITALY AT ALL. NOWHERE IS THIS TRUISM MORE TRUE THAN WHEN IT COMES TO PALERMO, THE MOST BEAUTIFULLY SITUATED CITY IN THE WORLD, DREAMING AWAY ITS LIFE IN THE CONCA D'ORO, THE EXQUISITE VALLEY THAT LIES BETWEEN TWO SEAS. OPPOSITE: THE TEATRO MASSIMO VITTORIO EMANUELE, IN THE CENTER OF PALERMO, IS THE LARGEST OPERA HOUSE IN ITALY.

PALAZZO VALGUARNERA-GANGI

GIUSEPPE *and* CARINE VANNI MANTEGNA DI GANGI

Palazzo Valguarnera-Gangi became the most spectacular palace in Palermo in the mid-eighteenth century when Pietro and Marianna Valguarnera, the Prince and Princess of Gangi, commissioned a number of artists and decorators to transform it into a folly of opulence and splendor. The palace, best known for having served as the set for the ball scene in Luchino Visconti's movie based on *The Leopard*, Giuseppe Tomasi di Lampedusa's novel, belongs to Prince Giuseppe Vanni Mantegna di Gangi—a direct descendant of the couple that created it—and his wife, Carine. After a period of neglect these interiors, thanks to the current princess, who has curated every detail, have undergone a major restoration that has lasted more than twenty years.

GIOACCHINO *and* NICOLETTA LANZA TOMASI

Thanks to its ten windows that open onto a majestic view of the sea, Palazzo Lanza Tomasi has extraordinary light, even for Palermo. Duke Gioacchino Lanza Tomasi, a cousin and adoptive son of the Prince of Lampedusa, the celebrated author of *The Leopard,* considers this "the house of my life." He and his wife, Nicoletta, are the custodians of Tomasi di Lampedusa's legacy. The author's library is the only room in the palace that has remained as he had left it. Other than that, the couple have made these graceful eighteenth-century interiors, complete with decorative murals, very much their own. The most important of these changes was restoring the palace's interiors. Palazzo Lanza Tomasi enshrines, within its walls, a second library, one that belonged to the duke's maternal grandfather, the Marquis Wenceslao Ramírez de Villa-Urrutia, a historian and a bibliophile who also served as a Spanish ambassador. Gioacchino Lanza Tomasi, a musical manager who has directed four opera theaters, has added his own books to the collection.

WINSPEARE FAMILY

The Salento peninsula, on the tip of Italy's heel, is the eastern edge of the western world, and the town of Depressa—with its pink stucco castle, its eighteenth-century church, and its 1,500 or so inhabitants—has earned the local moniker "Finibus Terrae": the ends of the earth. This remoteness speaks to Depressa's history. In an area plagued for centuries by Turkish incursions, invisibility was its strategy for survival. "Depressa is not a place one passes through," Elisabeth "Guky" Winspeare once said. "It's a final destination." Guky, Princess of Lichtenstein, first came to Salento in 1952 on vacation. When, some years later, Baron Riccardo "Dicky" Winspeare proposed to marry her and take her to live in his castle in Depressa, far away from her native Austria, she leaped at the opportunity. Dicky Winspeare was not only a charming and erudite cosmopolite. He was also a Salentino at heart. After inheriting Depressa in the 1930s he moved there from his native Naples with thousands of books, furniture, and family portraits. The central court, built within the original sixteenth-century walls, is partly his creation. To one end of it is the dog cemetery, where the baron found a way to align his love of dogs with his fondness for epigrams. Every Winspeare dog—including "Poor Giulia, Very Peculiar Dog of Apulia"—is honored here, under the shade of a few palms, with an epigram on a stone plaque.

GIOVANNI *and* LUCIA GUARINI

The facade of the Guarini palace in Scorrano, built during the seventeenth and eighteenth centuries over the remains of a medieval bastion, retains the forbidding massiveness of a military outpost. Life at the palace revolves around the inner courtyard. To the far end of the courtyard is Lucia Guarini's ceramic studio. Set between the palace's portal and the courtyard is a grand stone staircase leading up to the couple's apartment occupying the entire first floor, or piano nobile. "These interiors," says Giovanni Guarini, "have been lived in continuously by members of our family ever since the 1680s." The monumental entrance hall, adorned with stern-looking family portraits and a collection of ancient arms, including two small bronze cannons used by an ancestor during the historic naval fight of Lepanto in 1571, bears testimony to the family's military history. Lucia Guarini painted the walls in bright colors and introduced contemporary elements, including her ceramic artifacts, to the time-honed interiors. She restored the door cornices to their original eighteenth-century marble-inspired trompe l'oeil effect. Even the family chapel has been restored to new life. "This is a region of stark contrasts, with blinding sunlight and deep shadows," Lucia Guarini says. "Traditions are deeply felt here and one can never escape the past."

DEDICATIONS: To my wife, Atti, and my nephew Bu. –O. G.

To my mother. –M. C. C.

ACKNOWLEDGMENTS: Our gratitude goes to all the individuals in this book, who welcomed us into their homes and studios or into the museums they run. We would also like to thank the many people who helped us along the way with suggestions or generous hospitality. These include Stefano Aluffi-Pentini, Luisa Beccaria and Lucio Bonaccorsi, Annibale and Marida Berlingieri, Ana Luz Bravo, Viviana Calvisi, Patrizia Cavalli, Ida Corti, Lisa Corti, Allegra Hicks and Roberto Mottola d'Amato, Massimo D'Alessandro, Tonci and Barbara Foscari, Ileana Franchetti, Giuseppe Gallo and Cristina Lonardi, Idarica Gazzoni, Emanuela Iacoboaea, Lidia Berlingieri Leopardi, Holly Lueder and Venetia Sacret Young, Stefano Mancini and the crew at Il Giardino dei Tarocchi, Peter Benson Miller and Giovanni Panebianco, Tiziana Nasi, Luca Pignatelli, and Paola Santarelli. This book would not have been possible without our wonderful publisher, Charles Miers, and a lot of work from Mary Shanahan, who lent us her crisp and elegant vision, and Philip Reeser, who egged us on and kept us all on track. A special and loving thank-you to Atti Gili. This book is her work as much as it is ours. –M. C. C. and O. G.

First published in the United States of America in 2016 by

Rizzoli International Publications, Inc.
300 Park Avenue South
New York, NY 10010
www.rizzoliusa.com

Philip Reeser, Editor
Maria Pia Gramaglia, Production Manager
Elizabeth Smith, Copy Editor

ISBN: 978-0-8478-4927-7
Library of Congress Control Number: 2016938551

Distributed to the U.S. trade by Random House, New York

Printed and bound in Italy
2016 2017 2018 2019/ 10 9 8 7 6 5 4 3 2 1

DESIGNED BY MARY SHANAHAN